Italian Short Stories for Beginners Book 5

Over 100 Dialogues and Daily Used Phrases to Learn Italian in Your Car. Have Fun & Grow Your Vocabulary, with Crazy Effective Language Learning Lessons

www.LearnLikeNatives.com

www.LearnLikeNatives.com

© **Copyright 2020**

By Learn Like A Native

ALL RIGHTS RESERVED

No part of this book may be reproduced, stored in a retrieval system, or transmitted in any form or by any means, without the prior written permission of the publisher.

www.LearnLikeNatives.com

TABLE OF CONTENT

INTRODUCTION	5
CHAPTER 1 New Roommates	
/ Common everyday objects + possession	17
Translation of the Story	37
New Roommates	37
CHAPTER 2 A Day in the Life	
/ transition words	49
Translation of the Story	66
A Day in the Life	66
CHAPTER 3 The Camino Inspiration	
/ Numbers + Family	77
Translation of the Story	94
The Camino Inspiration	94
CONCLUSION	103
About the Author	109

www.LearnLikeNatives.com

www.LearnLikeNatives.com

INTRODUCTION

Before we dive into some Italian, I want to congratulate you, whether you're just beginning, continuing, or resuming your language learning journey. Here at Learn Like a Native, we understand the determination it takes to pick up a new language and after reading this book, you'll be another step closer to achieving your language goals.

As a thank you for learning with us, we are giving you free access to our 'Speak Like a Native' eBook. It's packed full of practical advice and insider tips on how to make language learning quick, easy, and most importantly, enjoyable. Head over to LearnLikeNatives.com to access your free guide and peruse our huge selection of language learning resources.

www.LearnLikeNatives.com

Learning a new language is a bit like cooking—you need several different ingredients and the right technique, but the end result is sure to be delicious. We created this book of short stories for learning Italian because language is alive. Language is about the senses—hearing, tasting the words on your tongue, and touching another culture up close. Learning a language in a classroom is a fine place to start, but it's not a complete introduction to a language.

In this book, you'll find a language come to life. These short stories are miniature immersions into the Italian language, at a level that is perfect for beginners. This book is not a lecture on grammar. It's not an endless vocabulary list. This book is the closest you can come to a language immersion without leaving the country. In the stories within, you will see people speaking to each other, going through daily life situations, and using the most common, helpful words and phrases in language.

www.LearnLikeNatives.com

You are holding the key to bringing your Italian studies to life.

Made for Beginners

We made this book with beginners in mind. You'll find that the language is simple, but not boring. Most of the book is in the present tense, so you will be able to focus on dialogues, root verbs, and understand and find patterns in subject-verb agreement.

This is not "just" a translated book. While reading novels and short stories translated into Italian is a wonderful thing, beginners (and even novices) often run into difficulty. Literary licenses and complex sentence structure can make reading in your second language truly difficult—not to mention BORING. That's why Italian Short

Stories for Beginners is the perfect book to pick up. The stories are simple, but not infantile. They were not written for children, but the language is simple so that beginners can pick it up.

The Benefits of Learning a Second Language

If you have picked up this book, it's likely that you are already aware of the many benefits of learning a second language. Besides just being fun, knowing more than one language opens up a whole new world to you. You will be able to communicate with a much larger chunk of the world. Opportunities in the workforce will open up, and maybe even your day-to-day work will be improved.

www.LearnLikeNatives.com

Improved communication can also help you expand your business. And from a neurological perspective, learning a second language is like taking your daily vitamins and eating well, for your brain!

How To Use The Book

The chapters of this book all follow the same structure:

- A short story with several dialogs
- A summary in Italian
- A list of important words and phrases and their English translation
- Questions to test your understanding
- Answers to check if you were right
- The English translation of the story to clear every doubt

www.LearnLikeNatives.com

You may use this book however is comfortable for you, but we have a few recommendations for getting the most out of the experience. Try these tips and if they work for you, you can use them on every chapter throughout the book.

1) Start by reading the story all the way through. Don't stop or get hung up on any particular words or phrases. See how much of the plot you can understand in this way. We think you'll get a lot more of it than you may expect, but it is completely normal not to understand everything in the story. You are learning a new language, and that takes time.

2) Read the summary in Italian. See if it matches what you have understood of the plot.

3) Read the story through again, slower this time. See if you can pick up the meaning of any words or phrases you don't understand

by using context clues and the information from the summary.

4) Test yourself! Try to answer the five comprehension questions that come at the end of each story. Write your answers down, and then check them against the answer key. How did you do? If you didn't get them all, no worries!

5) Look over the vocabulary list that accompanies the chapter. Are any of these the words you did not understand? Did you already know the meaning of some of them from your reading?

6) Now go through the story once more. Pay attention this time to the words and phrases you haven't understand. If you'd like, take the time to look them up to expand your meaning of the story. Every time you read over the story, you'll understand more and more.

7) Move on to the next chapter when you are ready.

Read and Listen

The audio version is the best way to experience this book, as you will hear a native Italian speaker tell you each story. You will become accustomed to their accent as you listen along, a huge plus for when you want to apply your new language skills in the real world.

If this has ignited your language learning passion and you are keen to find out what other resources are available, go to LearnLikeNatives.com, where you can access our vast range of free learning materials. Don't know where to begin? An excellent place to start is our 'Speak Like a Native' free eBook, full of practical advice and insider tips on how to make language learning quick, easy, and most importantly, enjoyable.

And remember, small steps add up to great advancements! No moment is better to begin learning than the present.

www.LearnLikeNatives.com

FREE BOOK!

Get the *FREE BOOK* that reveals the secrets path to learn any language fast, and without leaving your country.

Discover:

- The **language 5 golden rules** to master languages at will

- Proven **mind training techniques** to revolutionize your learning

- A complete step-by-step guide to **conquering any language**

www.LearnLikeNatives.com

www.LearnLikeNatives.com

www.LearnLikeNatives.com

CHAPTER 1
New Roommates / Common everyday objects + possession

STORIA

Oggi è giorno di trasferirsi all'università. Gli studenti del primo anno spostano le **loro** cose nel dormitorio.

Anna arriva all'università con i suoi genitori. La **sua** auto è carica di **scatoloni**. Anna porta con sé tutto ciò di cui ha bisogno per un anno di scuola. Parcheggiano al di fuori del dormitorio di Anna. L'edificio è un grande edificio in mattoni. Sembra noioso. Anna cerca di pensare positivo. Quest'anno sarà grandioso, si racconta.

La sua famiglia inizia a scaricare la macchina. Anna è molto preparata. Tirano fuori scatoloni pieni di cose sue. Suo fratello la aiuta a portare gli scatoloni fino alla stanza. La camera è piccola. Ci sono due letti. Anna avrà una coinquilina.

La prima scatola che Anna apre ha materiale scolastico. Mette i suoi **quaderni**, **matite** e **penne** sulla sua scrivania. La stanza non ha decorazioni, tranne che per una **televisione** sul muro. Anna organizza le sue cose nella stanza. Lei prende il suo **calendario** per appenderlo sul muro.

"Questo non è **mio**!" dice. È un calendario di belle donne.

"Questo è il **suo**", dice Anna, indicando suo fratello.

"Oh, scusa", dice suo fratello. Anna lo getta nel bidone della **spazzatura**. La famiglia ride.

Si sente bussare alla porta. Aprono la porta. Vedono una ragazza bionda. È con una donna più grande, sua madre.

"Ciao, sono Beatriz", dice la ragazza.

"Io sono Anna", dice Anna. "Immagino che siamo coinquiline!"

"Da dove vieni?" chiede Beatriz.

"Da qui vicino, solo un'ora a nord", dice Anna.

"Anch'io!" dice Beatriz.

Le ragazze si stringono la mano e sorridono. Beatriz porta i suoi scatoloni. Le famiglie aiutano le figlie a disfare i bagagli.

I primi giorni di scuola sono piacevoli. Anna si fa nuovi amici. Lei e Beatriz vanno d'accordo grande. Anna va alle sue nuove classi. Tutto è perfetto. Tranne una cosa. Alcuni degli effetti personali di Anna cominciano a scomparire. In primo luogo, non riesce a trovare il suo **pennello per il**

trucco. Poi, il giorno dopo, guarda lo **specchio**. Vede la sua **crema** ma manca il suo **profumo**. Quando ritorna dalla lezione quella sera, mette un po' di musica. Non c'è nessun suono. Il suo **altoparlante** è andato!

Chiede a Beatriz. "Beatriz", dice. "Ti manca qualcosa?"

"Sì!" dice Beatriz. "Il mio computer portatile. Sto impazzendo."

"Oh no!" dice Anna. "Anche a me mancano alcune cose."

Anna ha perduto tre oggetti ora. Chiama sua madre sul suo **cellulare**.

"Ciao, mamma", dice Anna.

"Ciao, tesoro", dice sua madre. "Come va la scuola?"

"Bene", dice Anna. "Ma le mie cose continuano a sparire."

"Cosa vuoi dire?" chiede sua madre. Anna dice a sua madre del profumo mancante, l'altoparlante mancante, e il pennello da trucco mancante.

"È così strano", dice sua madre. "Li hai portati da qualche parte?"

"No, mamma," dice Anna. "Non ho mai lasciato la stanza. Il resto del **sistema stereo** è qui. Compreso il mio **lettore mp3**."

"Chiudi la porta a chiave?" chiede sua madre.

"Sì, mamma!" dice Anna. "Ed è solo il profumo che è andato. Ho ancora tutti gli altri **trucchi**, **rossetto**, tutto!"

"Pensi che possa essere Beatriz?" chiede sua madre.

"Impossibile, anche a lei mancano degli oggetti", dice Anna.

"Ok, vai a controllare gli oggetti smarriti", dice la mamma di Anna.

"Ok! Devo andare", dice Anna.

Anna riaggancia il telefono. L'idea di sua madre è buona. Anna va al piano di sotto verso l'ufficio dormitorio. Chiede di vedere la scatola degli oggetti smarriti. La scatola è piena. Ci guarda attraverso. Trova **quaderni**, una **videocamera**, e anche un **pettine**. Ma non vede le sue cose. Cerca meglio. Vede un computer portatile.

"È **tuo**?" chiede, pensando a Beatriz. Lo tira fuori. Lo è. Prende il computer per darlo a Beatriz. Almeno ha trovato qualcosa.

Va di sopra. Dà il computer a Beatriz.

"Wow, Anna, è il **mio** computer!" dice Beatriz. "Grazie mille."

"Non c'è di che," dice Anna. "Sono così felice di aver trovato il **tuo** computer."

"Anch'io", dice Beatriz. "Hai trovato le tue cose?"

"No", dice Anna.

"Che sfortuna" dice Beatriz. Le ragazze vanno a dormire.

www.LearnLikeNatives.com

Il giorno dopo, Beatriz ha lezione. Anna rimane nella stanza del dormitorio. Sta lavorando a un progetto, utilizzando le **forbici** per tagliare le immagini da incollare su una **cartella**. Pensa ai suoi oggetti mancanti. Forse dovrebbe guardare nella stanza del dormitorio. Guarda ovunque. Poi si gira verso l'armadio di Beatriz. Lo apre e ci guarda dentro.

"Questo è mio!" dice Anna. Tira fuori il pennello da trucco. È scioccata. Perché il suo pennello è nell'armadio di Beatriz? Guarda più da vicino. Sotto una pila di **vestiti**, sente qualcosa di duro. Lo tira fuori. È la sua boccetta di profumo! Quando guarda più da vicino, trova anche il suo altoparlante.

"E 'stata Beatriz per tutto il tempo," dice Anna. Il **telefono** della stanza squilla. Anna risponde. E 'la mamma di Beatriz.

"Ciao, Anna", dice la mamma di Beatriz. "Come stai?"

"Bene", dice Anna. "Beatriz non c'è."

"Puoi dirle che ho chiamato?" chiede la mamma di Beatriz.

"Sì, ma, posso parlarti di una cosa?" chiede Anna.

"Certo", dice la mamma di Beatriz.

"Alcune delle mie cose sono scomparse", dice Anna. "E ne ho appena trovate molte nell'armadio di tua figlia."

"Oh, no", dice la mamma di Beatriz. "Devo dirti una cosa."

"Cosa?" dice Anna.

"Beatriz è una cleptomane", dice sua madre. "Prende le cose degli altri e poi le restituisce esattamente sette giorni dopo. Ti restituirà quegli oggetti entro domani."

"Cosa devo fare?" chiede Anna.

"Aspetta che li restituisca", dice sua madre.

"Ok", dice Anna.

"Grazie per la comprensione", dice la mamma di Beatriz.

RIASSUNTO

Anna e Beatriz sono coinquiline. E 'il loro primo anno all'università. Ottengono la loro stanza nel dormitorio dell'istituito. I loro genitori le aiutano con i bagagli. Vanno d'accordo. Durante la prima settimana, molti degli oggetti di Anna spariscono. Non riesce a trovarli da nessuna parte. Anche a Beatriz mancano alcuni oggetti. Anna guarda ovunque. Guarda negli oggetti smarriti, dove trova il computer mancante di Beatriz. Quando Beatriz non c'è, Anna guarda nel suo armadio e lì trova tutti i suoi oggetti. Chiama la mamma di Beatriz. Che le dice che Beatriz è una cleptomane.

LISTA DI VOCABOLI

loro	their
suo	her
Scatoloni	boxes
Mio	mine
Blocco note	notepads
Matita	pencils
Penna	pens
Televisione	television
Calendario	calendar

Suo	his
Spazzatura	trash can
Pennello da trucco	brush
Specchio	mirror
Crema	lotion
Profumo	perfume
Altoparlante/ casa	speaker
Computer	computer
Cellulare	cell phone
Sistema stereo	stereo system
Trucco	makeup

www.LearnLikeNatives.com

Rossetto	lipstick
Cuaderno	notebook
Videocamera	video camera
Pettine	comb
Mio	my
Tuo	your
Tuo	your
Forbici	scissors
Vestiti	clothes
Teléfono	telephone

www.LearnLikeNatives.com

DOMANDE

1) Come si conoscono Beatriz e Anna?

　　a) sono amiche da sempre

　　b) si incontrano in classe

　　c) sono coinquiline

　　d) frequentano la stessa scuola elementare

2) Quale di questi articoli non è scomparso?

　　a) pennello per il trucco

　　b) profumo

　　c) altoparlante

　　d) specchio

3) Cosa suggerisce la mamma di Anna?

    a) che Anna torni a casa

    b) che Anna affronti Beatriz

    c) che Anna compri un nuovo pennello da trucco

    d) che Anna guardi tra oggetti smarriti

4) Cosa trova Anna negli oggetti smarriti?

    a) il suo pennello da trucco

    b) Il computer di Beatriz

    c) una felpa

    d) il suo profumo

5) Cos'è successo alle cose di Anna?

a) Beatriz li ha presi e li ha messi nel suo armadio

b) Anna li ha persi

c) Anna li ha buttati via

d) nulla

RISPOSTE

1) Come si conoscono Beatriz e Anna?

c) sono coinquiline

2) Quale di questi articoli non è scomparso?

d) specchio

3) Cosa suggerisce la mamma di Anna?

d) che Anna guardi negli oggetti smarriti

4) Cosa trova Anna negli oggetti smarriti?

b) Il computer di Beatriz

5) Cos'è successo alle cose di Anna?

a) Beatriz li ha presi e li ha messi nel suo armadio

Translation of the Story

New Roommates

STORY

Today is move-in day at the university. First year students move **their** things into the dormitory.

Anna arrives to the university with her parents. **Her** car is loaded with **boxes**. Anna brings everything she needs for a year of school with her. They park outside of Anna's dormitory. The building is a big, brick building. It looks boring. Anna tries to think positive. This year will be great, she tells herself.

Her family begins to unload the car. Anna is very prepared. They take out boxes full of her things. Her brother helps her take the boxes up to the room. The room is small. There are two beds. Anna will have a roommate.

The first box Anna opens has school supplies. She puts her **notepads**, **pencils** and **pens** on her desk. The room has no decoration, except for a **television** on the wall. Anna organizes her things in the room. She takes her **calendar** out to put on the wall.

"This isn't **mine**!" she says. It is a calendar of pretty women.

"This is **his**," Anna says, pointing at her brother.

"Oh, sorry," says her brother. Anna throws it in the **trash can**. The family laughs.

There is a knock on the door. They open the door. A blonde girl stands outside. She is with an older woman, her mother.

"Hello, I'm Beatriz," says the girl.

"I'm Anna," says Anna. "I guess we are roommates!"

"Where are you from?" asks Beatriz.

"Nearby, just an hour north," says Anna.

"Me too!" says Beatriz.

The girls shake hands and smile. Beatriz brings her own boxes. The families help their daughters unpack.

The first days of school are nice. Anna makes new friends. She and Beatriz get along great. Anna goes to her new classes. Everything is perfect. However, one thing is wrong. Some of Anna's belongings begin to disappear. First, she can't find her **brush**. Then, the next day, she looks in the **mirror**. She sees her **lotion** but her **perfume** is missing. When she arrives from class that evening, she puts on some music. There is no sound. Her **speaker** is gone!

She asks Beatriz. "Beatriz," she says. "Are you missing anything?"

"Yes!" says Beatriz. "My laptop **computer**. I am freaking out."

"Oh no!" says Anna. "I am missing a few things, too."

Anna is missing three things now. She calls her mother on her **cell phone**.

"Hi, mom," says Anna.

"Hi, honey," says her mom. "How is school?"

"Fine," says Anna. "But my belongings keep disappearing."

"What do you mean?" asks her mom. Anna tells her mom about the missing perfume, the missing speaker, and the missing brush.

"That is so strange," says her mom. "Did you take them somewhere?"

"No, mom," says Anna. "I never left the room. The rest of the **stereo system** is here. My **mp3 player,** too."

"Do you lock your door?" asks her mom.

"Yes, mom!" says Anna. "And it's just the perfume that is gone. I still have all the other **makeup**, **lipstick**, everything!"

"Do you think it could be Beatriz?" asks her mom.

"No way, she is missing stuff too," says Anna.

"Ok, go check the lost-and-found," says Anna's mom.

"Ok! Gotta go," says Anna.

Anna hangs up the phone. Her mom's idea is good. She goes downstairs to the dormitory office. She asks to see the lost-and-found box. The box is full. She looks through it. She finds **notebooks**, a **video camera**, and even a **comb**. But does not see her things. She looks more. She sees a laptop **computer**.

"Is that **yours**?" she asks, thinking of Beatriz. She pulls it out. It is. She takes the computer to give to Beatriz. At least she finds something.

She goes upstairs. She gives Beatriz the computer.

"Wow, Anna, it's **my** computer!" says Beatriz. "Thank you so much."

"You're welcome," says Anna. "So glad I found **your** computer."

"Me too," says Beatriz. "Did you find any of your things?"

"No," says Anna.

"Bummer," says Beatriz. The girls go to sleep.

The next day, Beatriz has class. Anna stays in the dorm room. She works on a project, using **scissors** to cut pictures to glue on a **folder**. She thinks about her missing items. Maybe she should look in the dorm room. She looks everywhere. Then she turns to Beatriz's closet. She opens it. She looks inside it.

"This is mine!" says Anna. She pulls out her brush. She is shocked. Why is her brush in Beatriz's closet? She looks closer. Under a stack of **clothes**, she feels something hard. She pulls it out. It is her bottle of perfume! When she looks closer, she finds her speaker, too.

"It was Beatriz the whole time," says Anna. The room **telephone** rings. Anna answers. It is Beatriz's mom.

"Hi, Anna," says Beatriz's mom. "How are you?"

"Fine," says Anna. "Beatriz isn't here."

"Can you tell her I called?" asks Beatriz's mom.

"Yes, but, can I talk to you about something?" asks Anna.

"Sure," says Beatriz's mom.

"Some of my things have gone missing," says Anna. "And I just found many of them in **your** daughter's closet."

"Oh, no," says Beatriz's mom. "I need to tell you something."

"What?" says Anna.

"Beatriz is a kleptomaniac," says her mom. "She takes things and then returns them exactly seven days later. She will return those items to you by tomorrow."

"What do I do?" asks Anna.

"Just wait for her to return them," says her mom.

"Okay," says Anna.

"Thank you for understanding," says Beatriz's mom.

www.LearnLikeNatives.com

от*www.LearnLikeNatives.com*

CHAPTER 2
A Day in the Life / transition words

STORIA

Bey si sveglia in una stanza d'albergo. È stanca. Il suo corpo è stanco, **ma** la sua mente è più stanca. Si sente sola. I suoi amici e la sua famiglia non capiscono cosa vuol dire essere famosi. Ride. Vogliono diventare famosi. Vogliono trascorrere una giornata nella sua vita. La gente pensa che le celebrità si divertano tutto il giorno. Pensano che le celebrità abbiano tutto ciò che vogliono. **Tuttavia**, Bey sa che questo non è vero.

Perché la gente vuole essere famosa? pensa Bey. Si fa un caffè. I media la mostrano come un successo. La gente vuole il successo. Vogliono una vita perfetta. **Di conseguenza**, cercano di diventare famosi. Sa che la vita non è perfetta.

L'orologio dice che sono le sette. La sua giornata è piena. **Perciò** deve svegliarsi presto. Alcune persone pensano che le celebrità dormano fino a tardi. Ha molto da fare. Non c'è tempo per dormire fino a tardi. Sente il campanello.

"Ciao", dice Bey.

"Ciao, Bey", dicono le tre donne. Una donna è la sua stilista. Un'altra donna è la sua truccatrice. **Infine**, entra il parrucchiere. Apre la porta. Entrano. Cominciano a lavorare.

"Quale maglietta?" dice lo stilista.

"Di che colore è il rossetto?" chiede il truccatore.

"Perché hai dormito con i capelli così?" chiede il parrucchiere.

Il caffè di Bey è freddo. Si prepara un altro caffè. **Poi**, lei risponde a tutte le domande. Loro la aiutano. **Infine**, è pronta.

Lascia l'hotel alle 10 del mattino. Ci sono molte persone fuori. La aspettano. Quando esce, urlano. Scattano foto. Bey entra in una macchina. L'auto ha i finestrini scuri. Nessuno ci vede. Perciò può fare quello che vuole. Si rilassa. Il suo telefono squilla.

"pronto?" risponde.

"Bey, dove sei?" chiede il suo manager.

"In macchina", dice.

"Sei in ritardo!" dice il manager.

"Mi dispiace," ha detto Bey. Ha lezione di danza, lezioni di canto, e un servizio fotografico. Una giornata impegnativa. Il suo manager detta la sua giornata. Le dice cosa fare. Le dice quando andare. Si sente bloccata. Deve lavorare per rimanere famosa. Non può prendere una vacanza.

www.LearnLikeNatives.com

La macchina si ferma. **Prima**, Bey ha un servizio fotografico. E 'per una rivista. Una ragazza sistema il trucco di Bey. Lei è una sua fan. Sorride.

"Come stai?" chiede.

"Bene", dice Bey.

"Sono un tua fan", dice.

"Grazie", dice Bey.

"Canto anch'io", dice la ragazza. Trucca la faccia di Bey.

"Davvero?" chiede Bey. Si annoia.

"Sì. Voglio essere famosa!" dice la ragazza.

"Essere famosi porta a un sacco di lavoro!" dice Bey.

"Non mi importa!" disse la ragazza.

"Cosa fai stasera?" chiede Bey.

"Cena con il mio ragazzo, una passeggiata nel parco, magari visitiamo un museo", dice la ragazza.

"Devo lavorare, un concerto," dice Bey. "**Infatti**, Ne ho uno ogni sera. Non posso uscire al parco **perché** la gente mi riconosce. Non mi lasciano in pace."

"Oh", dice la ragazza. Finisce il trucco.

"**Per esempio**, non riesco a ricordare una visita ad un museo", dice Bey. Lei ha finito. Fa il servizio fotografico. Il suo vestito è stupendo. È bella e felice. Saluta e sale in macchina.

Adesso, Bey ha lezione di danza. Si esercita in una sala di danza. Il suo insegnante è un professionista. Si esercitano per il concerto. Il concerto di stasera è in uno stadio di New York. Dimentica i passi per la sua canzone più famosa. Si allena per due ore. **Senza dubbio**, conosce i passi.

Terzo, Bey ha lezioni di canto. Cantanti famosi hanno bisogno di lezioni. Le lezioni di canto li aiutano a cantare più facilmente. Questo è importante. **Dopo tutto**, cantare un concerto ogni sera è difficile.

Dopo la lezione di canto, mangia il suo pranzo. Il suo assistente glielo porta. Anche se è veloce, è sano. Ha un frullato e un'insalata. Presto dovrà prepararsi per il concerto.

Controlla il suo telefono. Bey ha un altro assistente. Questo assistente si occupa dei social media. Lei mette le foto su Instagram e Facebook. **Ma alla fine**, Bey ama controllare con i suoi occhi La sua nuova foto ha 1.000.000 di mi piace. Non male, pensa. Ha anche molti commenti. Alcuni sono cattivi, così Bey spegne il telefono. Cerca di essere positiva.

In macchina, Bey chiama i suoi amici. Parla con sua madre. Parla in macchina **poiché** non ha molto tempo. È stanca. Ha mal di testa. Forse può dormire. Guarda il telefono. È troppo tardi per dormire.

Mentre Bey si prepara, i fan aspettano. Fanno una fila fuori. Sono eccitati. Hanno pagato un sacco di soldi per i biglietti.

Ore le fa male la gola. Beve del tè caldo. **Se** lei non canta, i fan saranno dispiaciuti. Guarda il suo telefono. Ha una foto salvata per questi momenti. È una lettera.

"Cara Bey", dice.

"Tu sei la mia cantante preferita. Penso che tu sia incredibile. Voglio essere proprio come te quando cresco. Con affetto, Susy." È da un fan di 7 anni.

Bey si ricorda di lei. Sorride. Ci sono centinaia di ragazze come Susy al concerto. **Per questo motivo**, si esibisce.

Alla fine, il concerto finisce.

Sempre più fan chiedono l'autografo di Bey. Sorridono. Scattano foto sul loro telefono. Lei immagina le loro vite. Vanno alle feste. Vedono gli amici. Vanno ai ristoranti. **In ogni caso,** hanno la libertà. Lei è gelosa. **Pur** non essendo famosi, hanno una vita migliore.

Pensa alla ragazza del trucco di oggi. Si chiede, che cosa sta facendo ora? Bey pensa che forse smetterà di cantare.

All'improvviso, il suo telefono emette un suono.

È un promemoria per andare a letto. Domani è un altro giorno impegnativo.

RIASSUNTO

Bey è una celebrità. È una famosa cantante pop. La gente è gelosa della sua vita. Tuttavia, non è facile. La sua giornata inizia presto. I suoi tre assistenti vengono all'hotel. La preparano. Poi, ha una giornata impegnativa. Va a un servizio fotografico. La ragazza del trucco vuole essere famosa. Bey dice che non è così bello come pensa. Bey fa lezione di danza e di canto. Poi si prepara per il suo concerto. Ha mal di gola. Tuttavia, si esibisce per i suoi molti fan. Scatta foto e firma autografi. Si sente gelosa della vita normale dei suoi fan.

LISTA DI VOCABOLI

Ma	but
Comunque	however
Come risultato	as a result
Perciò	therefore
Infine	lastly
Poi	then
Allá fine	finally
Prima	first
Infatti	in fact
Perché	because
Per esempio	for example

www.LearnLikeNatives.com

Adesso	Now
Senza dubio	without a doubt
Dopo tutto	after all
Anche se	even though
Allá fine	ultimately
Così che	so
Poichè	since
Mentre	while
Se	if
Per questo motivo	for this reason
Eventualmente	Eventually.

In ogni caso	either way
Pur	despite
All'improvviso	all of a sudden

DOMANDE

1) Quale persona non è presente all'hotel di Bey?

    a) una truccatrice

    b) uno stilista

    c) un ammiratore

    d) un parrucchiere

2) Perché il manager di Bey la chiama?

   a) per chiedere dove si trova

   b) per licenziarla

   c) per congratularsi con lei

   d) per chiederle come sta

3) Che lavoro fa Bey?

   a) la ballerina

   b) è una pop star

   c) è una conduttrice di talk show

   d) è una fotografa

4) Cosa fa Bey per cantare meglio?

   a) beve del tè

b) frequenta lezioni di canto

c) prega

d) incrocia le dita

5) Cosa significa il suono del telefono alla fine della storia?

a) qualcuno sta chiamando

b) è il momento di prendere la medicina

c) una notifica da Instagram

d) è ora di andare a letto

RISPOSTE

1) Quale persona non viene all'hotel di Bey?

c) un ammiratore

2) Perché il manager di Bey la chiama?

a) per chiederle dove si trova

3) Che lavoro fa Bey?

b) è una pop star

4) Cosa fa Bey per cantare meglio?

b) frequenta lezioni di canto

5) Cosa significa il suono del telefono alla fine della storia?

d) è ora di andare a letto

Translation of the Story

A Day in the Life

STORY

Bey wakes up in a hotel room. She is tired. Her body is tired, **but** her mind is more tired. She feels alone. Her friends and family don't understand what it is like to be famous. She laughs. They want to be famous. They want to spend a day in her life. People think celebrities have fun all day. They think celebrities get anything they want. **However,** Bey knows this is not true.

Why do people want to be famous? Bey thinks. She makes a coffee. The media shows her as success. People want success. They want a perfect life. **As a result,** they try to become famous. She knows life is not perfect.

The clock says seven o'clock. Her day is busy. **Therefore**, she has to wake up early. Some people think celebrities sleep late. She has a lot to do. There is no time to sleep late. She hears the doorbell.

"Hello," says Bey.

"Hi, Bey," say the three women. One woman is her stylist. Another woman is her makeup artist. **Lastly**, the hairdresser enters. She opens the door. They go inside. They begin to work.

"Which shirt?" says the stylist.

"Which color of lipstick?" asks the makeup artist.

"Why did you sleep with your hair like that?" asks the hairdresser.

Bey's coffee is cold. She makes another coffee. **Then**, she answers all the questions. They help her. **Finally,** she is ready.

She leaves the hotel at 10 a.m. There are many people outside. They wait for her. When she goes out, they scream. They take pictures. Bey gets in a car. The car has dark windows. No one can see in. **Therefore,** she can do what she wants. She relaxes. Her phone rings.

"Hello?" she says.

"Bey, where are you?" asks her manager.

"In the car," she says.

"You're late!" says the manager.

"Sorry," said Bey. She has dance practice, voice lessons, and a photo shoot. A busy day. Her manager keeps her schedule. He tells her what to do. He tells her when to go. She feels stuck. She must work to stay famous. She can't take a vacation.

The car stops. **First**, Bey has a photo shoot. It is for a magazine. A girl puts makeup on Bey. She is a fan. She smiles.

"How are you?" she asks.

"Fine," says Bey.

"I am your fan," she says.

"Thank you," says Bey.

"I sing, too," the girl says. She powders Bey's face.

"Really?" asks Bey. She is bored.

"Yes. I want to be famous!" says the girl.

"Being famous is a lot of work!" says Bey.

"I don't care!" says the girl.

"What are you doing tonight?" asks Bey.

"Dinner with my boyfriend, a walk in the park, maybe visit a museum," says the girl.

"I have work, a concert," says Bey. "**In fact,** I have one every night. I can't go out to the park **because** people recognize me. They don't leave me alone."

"Oh," says the girl. She finishes the makeup.

"**For example**, I can't remember a visit to a museum," says Bey. She is finished. She takes her pictures. Her dress is glamorous. She looks beautiful and happy. She says goodbye and gets in the car.

Second, Bey has dance practice. She practices in a dance studio. Her teacher is professional. They practice for the concert. Tonight's concert is in a stadium in New York City. She forgets the dance for her most famous song. She practices for two hours. **Without a doubt**, she knows the dance.

Third, Bey has voice lessons. Famous singers need lessons. Voice lessons help them sing easily. This is important. **After all,** singing a concert every night is difficult.

After voice, she eats lunch. Her assistant brings it to her. Even though it is quick, it is healthy. She has a smoothie and a salad. Soon she must prepare for the concert.

She checks her phone. Bey has another assistant. This assistant does social media. She puts pictures on Instagram and Facebook. **Ultimately**, Bey likes to see for herself. Her new picture has 1,000,000 likes. Not bad, she thinks. It also has many comments. Some are mean, **so** Bey turns off her phone. She tries to be positive.

In the car, Bey calls her friends. She talks to her mother. She talks in the car **since** she doesn't have much time. She is tired. She has a headache. Maybe she can nap. She looks at her phone. It is too late to nap.

While Bey gets ready, fans wait. They make a line outside. They are excited. They paid a lot of money for the tickets.

Now her throat hurts. She drinks warm tea. **If** she can't sing, the fans will be sad. She looks at her phone. She has a picture saved for these moments. It is a letter.

"Dear Bey," it says.

"You are my favorite singer. I think you are amazing. I want to be just like you when I grow up. Love, Susy." It is from a 7-year-old fan. Bey remembers her. She smiles. There are hundreds of girls like Susy at the concert. **For this reason,** she performs.

Eventually, the concert ends.

More and more fans ask for Bey's autograph. They smile. They take pictures on their phone. She imagines their lives. They go to parties. They see friends. They go to restaurants. **Either way**, they have freedom. She is jealous. **Despite** not being famous, they have better lives.

She thinks of the makeup girl from today. She wonders, what is she doing now? Bey thinks maybe she will quit.

All of a sudden, her phone makes a sound.

It is a reminder to go to bed. Tomorrow is another busy day.

www.LearnLikeNatives.com

www.LearnLikeNatives.com

CHAPTER 3
The Camino Inspiration / Numbers + Family

Molly ama le avventure.

È la persona più coraggiosa della sua **famiglia**, anche più coraggiosa dei suoi **due fratelli**. Va spesso in campeggio nel bosco con la sua famiglia. Questo fine settimana vanno insieme in montagna. La luna splende e gli uccelli e gli animali sono tranquilli. Molly si siede con i suoi fratelli e sua **sorella** vicino al fuoco, parlando e giocando. Vedono un pipistrello volare sopra le loro teste.

"Ewww!" grida la sorella di Molly.

"Un pipistrello!" urla **uno** dei fratelli di Molly.

Poi, altri **tre** pipistrelli volano sopra le loro teste.

"Ahhh! chiamiamo **mamma** e **papà**!" grida l'altro fratello, John.

"È solo un pipistrello", dice Molly.

Arrivano altri pipistrelli, fino a quando ce ne sono **otto** che volano sopra le loro teste. La sorella e i fratelli di Molly si rifugiano nelle loro tende, spaventati a morte. Molly non si muove. Lei guarda come i pipistrelli volano in cerchio, ora **diciannove**, no, **venti**!

"Ciao, Molly", dice sua **madre**, camminando dietro suo **padre** verso il fuoco.

"Wow, ci sono sicuramente un sacco di pipistrelli intorno a questi boschi," dice suo padre. "Non hai paura?"

Molly scuote la testa negando, e guarda i pipistrelli volare nel cielo stellato della notte.

"Andiamo a cena!" dice. I suoi fratelli e sua sorella escono dalle loro tende. La famiglia mangia vicino al fuoco. Amano fare campeggio insieme.

Molly ha **ventidue** anni. Si è appena laureata al college, dove ha studiato ingegneria. Non ha trovato lavoro in un ufficio, quindi lavora nel suo negozio all'aperto. Risparmia il suo stipendio e parla del suo hobby preferito tutto il giorno: il campeggio.

Ogni sabato, Molly lavora al **secondo** piano, con tutte le tende, gli zaini e le provviste per il campeggio. Questo sabato, entra suo **cugino**.

"Ciao, Jim!" dice Molly, con un sorriso felice su suo viso.

"Molly! Dimenticavo che lavori qui", dice Jim, il figlio **trentenne** della **zia** di Molly.

"Come stanno zia Jane e **zio** Joe?" chiede Molly.

"Stanno bene. Questo fine settimana stanno visitando **nonna** Gloria a casa sua," dice Jim. "Sono qui per comprare alcuni oggetti da esterno per un viaggio."

"Oh, certo! Posso aiutarti. Cosa c'è sulla tua lista?" chiede Molly.

Jim mostra a Molly un pezzo di carta con una lista di **quindici** articoli. Uno zaino leggero, una stufa portatile, **quattro** paia di calzini caldi, bastoni da trekking, il sapone magico del Dr. Bronner, un coltellino da tasca e **diciotto** pasti da viaggio disidratati.

Wow, sembra un bel viaggio, pensa Molly.

"Dammi lo zaino più leggero che hai," dice Jim. "la versione più leggera di ogni oggetto, in realtà. Devo tenere il mio zaino sotto i **ventotto** chili."

"Per cosa stai comprando tutto questo?" chiede Molly, camminando con Jim verso una parete pieno di zaini di tutti i colori, grandi e piccoli.

"Farò un'escursione", dice Jim. "Attraverso la Spagna."

Jim prova i diversi zaini. Sceglie il preferito di Molly, uno zaino rosso con **sette** tasche, quattro sul retro e tre all'interno. Lo zaino è così leggero, che pesa appena un **chilo e mezzo**. Lo indossa sulle spalle mentre segue Molly nella sezione abbigliamento.

www.LearnLikeNatives.com

"Si chiama il Cammino di Santiago," dice Jim a Molly. Suo cugino le racconta dell'escursione. È un pellegrinaggio alla Cattedrale di Santiago de Compostela in Galizia. Si dice che San Giacomo sia sepolto nella chiesa.

Jim inizierà l'escursione a piedi, dal punto di partenza comune della Via Francese, Saint-Jean-Pied-de-Port. Da lì, sono circa **cinquecento** miglia fino a Santiago. Il pellegrinaggio è stato popolare fin dal Medioevo. Criminali e altre persone percorrevano il mammino in cambio di benedizioni. Al giorno d'oggi, la maggior parte delle persone viaggia a piedi. Alcune persone viaggiano in bicicletta. Alcuni pellegrini viaggiano anche a cavallo o su un asino. Il pellegrinaggio era religioso, ma ora molti lo fanno per viaggi o sport.

"Ho bisogno di viaggiare," dice Jim. "Ho bisogno di tempo per pensare e riflettere. Camminare 500 miglia può essere molto spirituale."

Molly aiuta Jim a trovare una giacca impermeabile e un paio di pantaloni che possono trasformarsi in pantaloncini. Sembra molto felice con la sua grande quantità di oggetti. Ha molto più cose nelle sue mani rispetto agli altri acquirenti. Farà un vero e proprio viaggio.

"Sono **trecentoquarantasette** dollari e **sessantasei** centesimi", dice Molly.

"Grazie, Molly", dice Jim.

Molly comincia a pensare. Vive a casa con i suoi **genitori**. Sua madre lavora come giudice nel tribunale locale e suo padre è un avvocato. Entrambi sono raramente a casa per cena. Rimangono occupati in ufficio fino a tardi. I suoi **fratelli** vivono con le loro famiglie a Seattle, a tre ore di distanza. È sola, senza un vero lavoro. Non ha nessuno che la fermi.

Sarà la vacanza perfetta. E forse deciderà cosa fare del resto della sua vita.

Perché no?

Quel giorno, Mollly decide che farà il Cammino di Santiago. A partire da settembre, tra tre mesi. Da sola.

RIASSUNTO

www.LearnLikeNatives.com

Una giovane donna di nome Molly ama l'aria aperta. Lei e la sua famiglia fanno spesso campeggio insieme. Lei lavora in un negozio all'aperto, mentre cerca un lavoro post l'università. Suo cugino Jim visita per prepararsi per un viaggio. Sta andando a fare un'escursione al Camino de Santiago e ha bisogno di rifornimenti. Molly lo aiuta a comprare uno zaino, scarpe e tutto il resto di cui ha bisogno. Alla fine, decide di andare lei stessa a fare il Camino.

LISTA DI VOCABOLI

Famiglia	family
Due	two
Fratello	brother

Sorella	sister
Uno/una	one
Tre	three
Mamma	mom
Papá	dad
Otto	eight
Diciannove	nineteen
Venti	twenty
Madre	mother
Padre	father
Ventidue	twenty-two

secondo	second
Primo/ Prima	cousin
Trenta	thirty
Figlio	son
Zia	aunt
Zio	uncle
Nonna	grandma
Quindici	fifteen
Quattro	four
Diciotto	eighteen
Ventotto	twenty-eight

Sette	seven
Due e mezzo	two-and-a-half
Cinquecento	five hundred
Trecento	three hundred
Quarantasetta	forty-seven
Sessantasei	sixty-six
Genitori	parents
Fratelli	siblings

DOMANDE

1) Cosa ha studiato Molly all'università?

    a) cosmetica

    b) letteratura

    c) ingegneria

    d) marketing

2) Quanti fratelli ha Molly?

    a) uno

    b) due

    c) tre

    d) quattro

3) In che modo Jim è imparentato con Molly?

a) è il fratello di Molly

b) è il cugino di Molly

c) è il nonno di Molly

d) è il papà di Molly

4) Che cos'è il Cammino di Santiago?

    a) un pellegrinaggio

    b) una città

    c) una chiesa

    d) una vacanza

5) Da dove viene Molly?

    a) negli Stati Uniti

    b) in Inghilterra

c) in Australia

d) in Francia

RISPOSTE

1) Cosa ha studiato Molly all'università?

    c) ingegneria

2) Quanti fratelli ha Molly?

    c) tre

3) In che modo Jim è imparentato con Molly?

    b) è il cugino di Molly

www.LearnLikeNatives.com

4) Che cos'è il Cammino di Santiago?

    a) un pellegrinaggio

5) Da dove viene Molly?

    a) negli Stati Uniti

www.LearnLikeNatives.com

Translation of the Story

The Camino Inspiration

Molly loves adventures.

She is the bravest member of her **family**, even braver than her **two brothers**. She often goes camping with her family in the woods. This weekend, they go to the mountain together. The moon shines and the birds and animals are quiet. Molly sits with her brothers and her **sister** by the fire, talking and playing. They see a bat fly over their heads.

"Ewww!" shouts Molly's sister.

"A bat!" yells **one** of Molly's brothers.

Then, **three** more bats fly over their heads.

"Ahhh! Let's get **mom** and **dad**!" shouts the other brother, John.

"It's only a bat," says Molly.

More bats arrive, until there are **eight** flying overhead. Molly's sister and brothers disappear into their tents, scared out of their wits. Molly does not move. She watches as the bats circled, now **nineteen**, no, **twenty**!

"Hi, Molly," says her **mother**, walking up behind her **father** to the campfire.

"Wow, there sure are a lot of bats around these woods," says her dad. "Aren't you scared?"

Molly shook her head no, and watched the bats fly off into the starry night sky.

"Let's eat dinner!" she said. Her brothers and sister come out of their tents. The family eats by the fire. They love to camp together.

Molly is **twenty-two**. She just graduated from college, where she studied engineering. She has not found a job in an office, so she works at her local outdoor store. She saves her paycheck and gets to talk about her favorite hobby all day: camping.

Every Saturday, Molly works on the **second** floor, with all of the tents, backpacks, and camping supplies. This Saturday, in walks her **cousin**.

"Hi, Jim!" says Molly, a happy smile on her face.

"Molly! I forgot you work here," says Jim, the **thirty**-year-old **son** of Molly's **aunt** Jane.

"How are Aunt Jane and **Uncle** Joe?" asks Molly.

"They're good. This weekend they are visiting **Grandma** Gloria at her house," says Jim. "I'm here to buy some outdoor goods for a trip."

"Oh, sure! I can help you. What is on your list?" Molly asks.

Jim shows Molly a piece of paper with a list of **fifteen** items. A light backpack, a portable stove, **four** pairs of warm socks, hiking poles, Dr. Bronner's magic soap, a pocket knife, and **eighteen** dehydrated trail meals.

Wow, this sounds like quite a trip, thinks Molly.

"Gimme the lightest backpack you have," says Jim. "The lightest everything, actually. I have to keep my pack under **twenty-eight** pounds."

"What are you buying all of this for?" asks Molly, walking with Jim over to a wall filled with backpacks of all colors, large and small.

"I'm going to hike," says Jim. "Across Spain."

Jim tries on the different backpacks. He chooses Molly's favorite, a red backpack with **seven** pockets, four on the back and three inside. The pack is so light, it hardly weighs **two-and-a-half** pounds. He wears it on his shoulders as he follows Molly to the clothing section.

"It's called the Camino de Santiago," Jim tells Molly. Her cousin tells her about the hike. It is a pilgrimage to the Cathedral of Santiago de Compostela in Galicia. People say that Saint James is buried in the church.

Uncle Jim will be walking the hike from the common starting point of the French Way, Saint-Jean-Pied-de-Port. From there, it is about **five hundred** miles to Santiago. The pilgrimage has been popular since the Middle Ages. Criminals and other people walked the way in exchange for blessings. Nowadays, most travel by foot. Some people travel by bicycle. A few pilgrims even travel on a horse or donkey. The pilgrimage was religious, but now many do it for travel or sport.

"I need to travel," says Jim. "I need time to think and reflect. Walking 500 miles can be very spiritual."

Molly helps Jim find a waterproof jacket and a pair of pants that can unzip to be shorts. He seems very happy with his large bag of things. He has much more in his hands than the other shoppers. He is going on a real trip.

"That will be **three hundred forty-seven** dollars and **sixty-six** cents," says Molly.

"Thanks, Molly," says Jim.

Molly begins to think. She lives at home with her **parents**. Her mother works as a judge in the local courthouse and her father is a lawyer. They are both rarely home for dinner. They stay busy at the office until late. Her **siblings** live with their families in Seattle, three hours away. She is alone, with no real job. She has no one to stop her.

It will be the perfect vacation. And maybe she will decide what to do with the rest of her life.

Why not?

That day, Mollly decides that she will do the Camino de Santiago. Starting in September, three months from now. Alone.

www.LearnLikeNatives.com

CONCLUSION

You did it!

You finished a whole book in a brand new language. That in and of itself is quite the accomplishment, isn't it?

Congratulate yourself on time well spent and a job well done. Now that you've finished the book, you have familiarized yourself with over 500 new vocabulary words, comprehended the heart of 3 short stories, and listened to loads of dialogue unfold, all without going anywhere!

Charlemagne said "To have another language is to possess a second soul." After immersing yourself in this book, you are broadening your horizons and opening a whole new path for yourself.

www.LearnLikeNatives.com

Have you thought about how much you know now that you did not know before? You've learned everything from how to greet and how to express your emotions to basics like colors and place words. You can tell time and ask question. All without opening a schoolbook. Instead, you've cruised through fun, interesting stories and possibly listened to them as well.

Perhaps before you weren't able to distinguish meaning when you listened to Italian. If you used the audiobook, we bet you can now pick out meanings and words when you hear someone speaking. Regardless, we are sure you have taken an important step to being more fluent. You are well on your way!

Best of all, you have made the essential step of distinguishing in your mind the idea that most often hinders people studying a new language. By approaching Italian through our short stories and dialogs, instead of formal lessons with just grammar and vocabulary, you are no longer in the 'learning' mindset. Your approach is much more similar to an osmosis, focused on speaking and using the language, which is the end goal, after all!

So, what's next?

This is just the first of five books, all packed full of short stories and dialogs, covering essential, everyday Italian that will ensure you master the basics. You can find the rest of the books in the series, as well as a whole host of other resources, at LearnLikeNatives.com. Simply add the book to your library to take the next step in your language learning journey. If you are ever in need of new ideas or direction, refer to our 'Speak Like a Native' eBook, available to you for free at LearnLikeNatives.com, which clearly outlines practical steps you can take to continue learning any language you choose.

We also encourage you to get out into the real world and practice your Italian. You have a leg up on most beginners, after all—instead of pure textbook learning, you have been absorbing the sound and soul of the language. Do not underestimate the foundation you have built reviewing the chapters of this book. Remember, no one feels 100% confident when they speak with a native speaker in another language.

One of the coolest things about being human is connecting with others. Communicating with someone in their own language is a wonderful gift. Knowing the language turns you into a local and opens up your world. You will see the reward of learning languages for many years to come, so keep that practice up!. Don't let your fears stop you from taking the chance to use your Italian. Just give it a try, and remember that you will make mistakes. However, these mistakes will teach you so much, so view every single one as a small victory! Learning is growth.

www.LearnLikeNatives.com

Don't let the quest for learning end here! There is so much you can do to continue the learning process in an organic way, like you did with this book. Add another book from Learn Like a Native to your library. Listen to Italian talk radio. Watch some of the great Italian films. Put on the latest CD from Pavarotti. Take cooking lessons in Italian. Whatever you do, don't stop because every little step you take counts towards learning a new language, culture, and way of communicating.

www.LearnLikeNatives.com

www.LearnLikeNatives.com

Learn Like a Native is a revolutionary **language education brand** that is taking the linguistic world by storm. Forget boring grammar books that never get you anywhere, Learn Like a Native teaches you languages in a fast and fun way that actually works!

As an international, multichannel, language learning platform, we provide **books, audio guides and eBooks** so that you can acquire the knowledge you need, swiftly and easily.

Our **subject-based learning**, structured around real-world scenarios, builds your conversational muscle and ensures you learn the content most relevant to your requirements.
Discover our tools at *LearnLikeNatives.com*.

When it comes to learning languages, we've got you covered!